BRITISH MUSEUM READING ROOM

THE BRITISH MUSEUM

A GUIDE

TO ITS PUBLIC SERVICES

Published by

THE TRUSTEES OF THE BRITISH MUSEUM

1970

First published in 1962

by THE TRUSTEES OF THE BRITISH MUSEUM

© 1970, second edition

SBN 7141 0026 9

Printed in Great Britain by
W. & J. Mackay & Co Ltd
Chatham, Kent

INTRODUCTORY NOTE TO FIRST EDITION
1962

by Sir Frank Francis, K.C.B., M.A., D.LITT., F.S.A., F.M.A.

One of my illustrious predecessors began an introduction to a book about the British Museum Library with the following words: 'The British Museum is, next to the British Navy, the national institution which is held in most universal respect abroad'. These words suggest that the British Museum is not appreciated in Britain as it should be and that there may well be some truth in the complaint which is heard from time to time that the British Museum does not make its services well enough or widely enough known. This booklet is our first attempt to provide the answer to this complaint.

The public services of the British Museum, as will appear from the pages which follow, are multifarious. They are organised partly by the Director's Office and partly by the individual Departments. The former is responsible for the administration of the Museum as a whole and for the services which cover all the Departments such as, for example, the production of the popular guide books, picture postcards, Christmas cards, the making of casts, photographic services, and lecture tours; individual Departments serve the public by providing exhibitions in the public galleries and by giving advice and information on specialised topics in the students' rooms.

The British Museum is both a library and a museum. This unusual combination of functions is due to the breadth and comprehensiveness of the foundation collections which were brought together as the result of the will of Sir Hans Sloane in 1753. The collections of antiquities aim at providing the material evidence for the history of the cultures of the world, and closely linked with the British Museum Library they form unrivalled instruments of scholarship.

3

Universality of material involves the application of universality of use: every kind of service to every kind of person. The collections have been organised with this obligation in view and they are available, *in toto*, to the public, whether in the exhibition galleries or in the students' rooms. Here the student, however advanced or however humble, can rely on finding material he needs from moment to moment; he can check his references; he can check the actual objects against the printed word, and illuminate the printed word by reference to the actual objects.

The catalogues prepared by the various Departments of the Museum have always been famous for their range and their scholarship. They are supported by specialised monographs on individual objects, or on subjects represented in the collections. Many of the departmental guides available before the last war have had to undergo revision as a result of changes during and since the war, but they are being reinforced by popular handbooks on separate subjects compiled by experts but designed for the non-expert reader. A list of all such publications is available on demand.

The present buildings of the British Museum, magnificent though they are, were designed at a time when the services expected from such an institution were very different from what they should be today. For this reason our students' rooms and the reading rooms in the library departments are not as well designed or as well co-ordinated as we should like. None the less very special efforts have been made, especially since the last war, to provide satisfactory facilities for students in all the departments.

I hope this booklet will make clear that the services of the expert staff are always available for genuine enquirers and that we are doing our best to provide good conditions under which the collections can be viewed and studied.

INTRODUCTORY NOTE TO SECOND EDITION
1970
by Sir John Wolfenden, C.B.E., M.A., D.LITT., LL.D.

Since the first edition of this Guide was published in 1962 a good many changes have occurred in the British Museum. So this revised edition has been prepared, to bring the information up to date.

The British Museum exists to serve a broad spectrum of users. The Keepers of the various collections are distinguished scholars; their expert colleagues from all over the world come to consult them and their collections; individual researchers are given access to specialised material for a wide variety of purposes; parties of school-children are received daily; and the general public, from Britain and abroad, visit the Museum's exhibition galleries in ever-increasing numbers. It is not easy to meet the needs of this variety of users in a building which is almost as inflexible as it is impressive. But by continual improvisation every attempt is constantly made to provide the services which each category of visitor requires.

It seems likely that within the next few years the traditional unity of the Museum departments and the Library departments may be dissolved, though not, it is to be hoped, their physical proximity. In that event, a good deal of this Guide will need to be re-written. In the meantime we offer this present edition as a factual and up-to-date statement of the services which the British Museum sets out to provide.

12th November, 1969.

CONTENTS

THE BRITISH MUSEUM

ADMISSION FREE

Exhibitions Open:

Weekdays   10 a.m. to 5 p.m.

Sundays   2.30 to 6 p.m.

CLOSED ON CHRISTMAS DAY, BOXING DAY AND GOOD FRIDAY

THE BRITISH MUSEUM, incorporated by an Act of Parliament in 1753, is the national museum of antiquities and ethnography and also the national library of the United Kingdom. In addition it houses the national collection of drawings by Old Masters, of British drawings and of prints. The natural history collections were removed to South Kensington between 1830 and 1883 and between 1904 and 1905 a repository for newspapers was built at Colindale, London, N.W.9, where additional buildings, including a reading room, were provided in 1932. In April 1966 the British Museum assumed responsibility for the Patent Office Library, which is now the National Reference Library of Science and Invention divided into the Holborn Division and the Bayswater Division. The reading rooms, the open-access collection of modern scientific literature and the reader services of this library are to be found at Holborn and at Bayswater.

Facilities for students in the main British Museum building have grown with the gradual enlargement of the building itself. When the Museum was first opened, a room was provided for students using the library but it was not until 1831 that a Reading Room was open every week-day.

In addition to the main Reading Room, which accommodates about 390 readers, the Department of Printed Books offers accommodation in the North Library—reconstructed in 1937—for special research, and in the Map Room and State Paper Room. Students' Rooms are available in the other Library Departments

(Manuscripts, and Oriental Printed Books and Manuscripts) and in the Departments of Prints and Drawings, Coins and Medals, Egyptian Antiquities, Western Asiatic Antiquities, Prehistoric and Romano-British Antiquities, Oriental Antiquities, and Ethnography. Other services offered by the Museum include the publication of specialised catalogues of the collections, the preparation of which has, from the beginning, been one of the main tasks of the senior staff.

These services are systematically discussed in the following pages under departmental headings.

The British Museum advances learning by the provision of materials and facilities for research, and by the encouragement of the study of literature, history, archaeology, art and science. Public use of the collections, which illustrate every aspect of the history of civilisation, is afforded by the Reading Rooms and services in the Library Departments; by Students' Rooms in other departments; by exhibition of select material in the Public Galleries; by public lecture-tours; by the publication of catalogues, guide books and reproductions; by photographic services; by the supply of casts; and by information given in response to personal inquiry.

General Information

THE MAIN ENTRANCE to the British Museum is in Great Russell Street, London, WCI, which connects Tottenham Court Road with Southampton Row and runs parallel to New Oxford Street. The nearest Underground stations are Holborn (Kingsway) and Tottenham Court Road.

The *North Entrance* is in Montague Place, facing the Senate House of London University. The nearest Underground stations are Russell Square and Goodge Street.

The following bus routes have stops near the Museum: 1, 1a, 7, 8, 8b, 14, 19, 19a, 22, 24, 25, 29, 38, 55, 68, 73, 77, 77a, 77b, 77c, 78, 78b, 134, 163, 170, 172, 176, 188, 188a, 196.

Invalid chairs: Invalid chairs are kept at the Main and North Entrances. Apply to the Superintendent on duty.

Hours of Opening: The hours of opening are 10 a.m. to 5 p.m. on weekdays and 2.30 to 6 p.m. on Sundays. The Museum is closed on Christmas Day, Boxing Day and Good Friday.

For information on the students' rooms and Reading Rooms in the various departments, including those Reading Rooms not situated in the main British Museum building, see the relevant sections of this book. Photographs of important objects not on view in the galleries may generally be seen in the students' room of the department.

The Director's Office: Just beyond the Publications Gallery to the left of the main entrance.

This office deals with administration, public services, publications, photographic services, guide lectures, etc.

Information Desk: The information officer at the enquiry desk in the front hall of the Museum will give information, or direct visitors.

Lifts: There is a public lift in the main entrance hall which serves the upper floors of the main building. A lift at the North entrance serves all floors of the King Edward VII building and provides access to the upper galleries of the main building.

Telephones: There are public telephones at the rear of the Main Entrance Hall.

Tea Room: The Tea Room is open daily from 10.30 a.m. to 4.30 p.m. except Sunday when it is open from 3 to 5.15 p.m. and can be reached through the Early Greek and Bronze Age Rooms.

Reading and Students' Rooms: Admission to the Reading and Students' Rooms of the Library Departments is normally granted for purposes of research and reference which cannot be satisfied elsewhere.

To use the Students' Rooms of the Department of Prints and Drawings, the Departments of Antiquities and the Department of Coins and Medals, application should be made direct to the appropriate departmental office.

GUIDE LECTURES

Information on scheduled lectures, twice daily at 11.30 a.m. and 3 p.m., as well as 15 minute lunchtime lectures from 1.00 to 1.15 p.m., can be obtained at the main enquiry desk. Members of the public who wish to attend are asked to assemble at the Guide Lecturer's notice board in the Main Entrance Hall (Great Russell Street), at the time stated. A detailed monthly programme will be posted to any enquirer on request.

Some fifty different lectures every month cover a wide range of the collections in the Museum; special lecture tours for a limited number of parties from educational institutions and similar organisations may be arranged by writing if ample notice is given before the date of the proposed visit.

All lecture tours are free.

PUBLICATIONS

The publications of the Museum can be divided into monographs on subjects represented in the collections of one of its departments, the catalogues of the collections which are published both for use in the Museum and the respective students' room and for sale to the public, and an increasing number of popular titles. A Guide to the Museum and guides to particular collections are also issued. A Guide Map showing the various galleries and rooms in colour is on sale.

The British Museum Quarterly deals with current acquisitions and research concerning the Museum's collections. Copies (5s. per part, 5s. 9d. post free) can be purchased in the Museum or by post by placing an annual or five-yearly subscription.

Postcards: Over 1000 postcards are on sale, showing objects of the antiquities departments or illustrations from books or manuscripts. Christmas cards and greeting cards are also published. A series of old maps in colour (Saxton's County Maps of England and Wales) are on sale. Other pictorial reproductions include a facsimile of the Shakespeare Deed, water-colour reproductions, etc.

A list of postcards, Christmas cards, greetings cards and 35 mm. transparencies may be had on request.

Plaster casts and replicas from Sculptures: The British Museum has facilities for making casts from objects in its collections. Illustrated lists are issued free of charge.

The list of 'Books in Print' will be sent free on request to any enquirer.

PHOTOGRAPHY

REGULATIONS

1. Applications must be made in ink, and in block letters.
2. The Photographic Service undertakes only photographic work connected with the Museum's collections.

3. Orders can be accepted by post or in person, either in the Department concerned, or at the Photographic Enquiry Counter in the Director's Office.
4. The fullest description available should be given, including pressmarks, dates of publication, or catalogue references wherever appropriate. Omission of references can lead to delay in the handling of an order.
5. The Departments of the Museum have a large collection of negatives from which contact prints and enlargements can be supplied.
6. Photographs of objects for which no negatives exist can be supplied, subject to Departmental approval.
7. Any special instructions must be stated clearly on the order form.
8. Wherever possible applications should be made on the official form which is available throughout the Museum. Postal requests should be sent to the Photographic Service, The British Museum, London, W.C.1.
9. Remittances should be made payable to the Trustees of the British Museum, and sent to the Accounts Section.
10. All photographs (as defined in the Copyright Act 1956) are the copyright of the Trustees of the British Museum and may not be reproduced without permission. Applications for permission should be made in writing with a statement of the nature of the application. The Trustees reserve the right to make a charge for reproduction.
11. Prints are available on application.

PHOTOGRAPHY BY VISITORS

Gallery Photography (prices are subject to alteration)
1. Hand cameras, not requiring a stand or special lighting, may be used in the Exhibition Galleries without special permission or fee. (Photography in the Reading Room is not permitted.)
2. For photography in the Galleries requiring tripod or special equipment, application must be made at least 48 hours beforehand in writing, indicating the objects and the Gallery in which they are situated. Any lighting required must be supplied by the applicant and his application should indicate the type of plug and amperage lead to be used. This photography must be carried out between the hours of 9 a.m. and 10 a.m., Monday to Friday. The fee for the service provided is 10s. 0d. an hour, payable at the Director's Office on completion of photography.
3. No exposed flashlight or other inflammable material may be brought into the Museum. Flash bulbs and electronic flash may be used.

Studio Photography (prices are subject to alteration)
4. The Museum Photographic Service undertakes every kind of photography connected with the collections, but the Studio may be used by *professional photographers,* subject to approval. Applications should be addressed to the

Photographic Service on the official form provided. Full details of the proposed work, and the Departmental reference numbers of the objects must be stated.

5. The Studio is open from 10.30 a.m. to 12.30 p.m. and 2.0 p.m. to 4.0 p.m., Monday to Friday, excepting Public Holidays.

6. Normal lighting only is provided in the Studio and any special equipment must be provided by the photographer himself.

7. The fee for the use of the Studio is £1 an hour, for up to one day. If two or more consecutive days are taken the fee is £2 2s. 0d. a day.

8. Permission may be given for work to be done elsewhere in the Museum on similar conditions. In such cases, charges will be made appropriate to the labour and lighting involved.

Rapid Copies (prices are subject to alteration)

1. Applications from readers for copying by this service can be accepted *only when made in person* in the Reading Room, North Library, or Students' Room of Oriental Printed Books. Orders will be accepted up to half an hour before the closing of the above centres.

2. Books from which pages are to be copied must be handed with the official order form to the Superintendent of the Reading Room, North Library or Students' Room of the Oriental Printed Book Department, with the pages marked by bookmarkers which are to be obtained from the above centres.

3. ALL payments must be made in advance on handing in the form. (Please give the exact money if possible).

4. Fixed price per copy 1s. 0d. Maximum size for one page or two facing pages (binding permitting) is 14" × 9" (35 × 23 cm).

5. Price for Inland postage and packing, if required, is 1s. 6d. for a maximum of 40 copies, and 2s. 6d. for 41–100 copies. Thereafter charges will be according to the current PARCEL POST rate.

Overseas fixed rate for a maximum of 40 copies is 2s. 6d., and 4s. 0d. for 41–100 copies. Thereafter charges are at the current parcel post rate.

Registration or Insurance if required 3s. extra (for up to £100 in value).

Airmail also will be charged extra, at the current rate.

N.B. *Orders awaiting collection will be held for up to 14 days after which they will be posted to the address given, and postage charged.*

6. Copies can be supplied only in accordance with the provisions of the Copyright Act, 1956, the Copyright (Libraries) Regulations, 1957, and the Copyright (International Conventions) Order, 1957, and amending orders.

For British publications and for those of many foreign countries, the written permission of the copyright owner is normally required before reproducing *any work first published, or whose author was living, within the last 50 years.* If, however, the declaration printed on the office order forms is signed by the person for whom the copy is to be made the following may be supplied without such permission:

(*a*) ONE article in any one issue of a periodical.

(*b*) PART of a work of which the copyright owner cannot be discovered by reasonable enquiry.

In certain other cases, a copy may be supplied to a library but not to an individual applicant.

(*c*) Extracts from any work other than music, totalling not more than one tenth of the whole work, provided that, in addition:

(i) if a single extract it does not exceed 4,000 words,
(ii) if several extracts no one extract exceeds 3,000 words and the total does not exceed 8,000 words.

7. The Trustees reserve the right to reject an application at their discretion.

National Reference Library of Science and Invention Photocopy service

Both Divisions of the National Reference Library of Science and Invention can supply photocopies from their holdings subject to the provisions of the Copyright Act, 1956.

Orders may be delivered personally to either the Holborn Division or the Bayswater Division of the Library, or may be sent by post to: The National Reference Library of Science and Invention (Holborn Division), Photocopy Section, 25 Southampton Buildings, Chancery Lane, London, W.C.2.

Orders delivered personally should be handed in to one of the photocopy order counters. At the Holborn Division these are situated at the east end of the ground floor in the main Library and in the Foreign Patents section in the Chancery House Annexe. At the Bayswater Division the counter is in the reading room. When the photocopy sections are closed orders may be handed in at the Central Information Desks; customers may either call back for the copies or have them sent by post.

Orders must be made on one of the N.R.L.S.I.'s printed forms, which are available free on request to the Photocopy Section, or on a Patent Office Deposit Account Order Form.

While-you-wait service

Electrostatic (e.g. Xerox) copies can usually be supplied within a few minutes to personal callers between 9.30 a.m. and 4.45 p.m., Monday to Friday. The number of pages that can be copied immediately is limited by the demand being made on the service at the time. The item to be copied should be taken to the nearest order counter and one of the cash order forms filled in. (Deposit Account forms may be used for the while-you-wait service).

COST

The charge for electrostatic copies is 9*d.* per page for most page sizes. These give good black on white reproduction of text and line illustrations. All photo-copying is done this way unless otherwise specified in the order. Arrangements can be made to supply Photostat copies (the delivery period is somewhat longer) at a charge of 1*s.* 6*d.* per page for most items.

PAYMENT

Payment must be made in advance. The recommended method is by Deposit Account, but payment by cash, postal order, money order, or cheque is accepted; cheques, etc., should be made out to 'The British Museum'.

To open a Deposit Account, the customer deposits with the Patent Office a sum of money, minimum twenty pounds (£20). From then until the sum is exhausted, the cost is defrayed against the Deposit Account whenever he orders photocopies. When the amount in the account is running low the customer is notified. Since this system obviates the need to send money with each order, it also obviates the need to calculate in advance the exact cost of each order. It is, however, essential to submit each order on one of the special forms which are issued to each Deposit Account holder. No service fee is charged for the Deposit Account, which may also be used for purchasing copies of British Patent specifications from the Patent Office. Full details of the system can be obtained from: The Patent Office, Sale Branch, Block C, Station Square House, St. Mary Cray, Orpington, Kent.

SKETCHING

1. Sketching with pencil, crayon or fountain-pen is freely permitted in the exhibition galleries of the British Museum provided that visitors observe the following conditions:

(a) They must not cause any obstruction by getting in the way of other visitors or by laying their personal belongings on the exhibits or on cases. They are not permitted to touch the exhibits.

(b) They may bring stools and small easels for use in the large sculpture galleries on the ground floor, subject to their not obstructing the view or access of other visitors. A limited number of stools are available on loan from the Hall Superintendent. Stools must be returned after use to the Hall Superintendent's office.

(c) Except in the large sculpture galleries on the ground floor not more than one person at a time may work on any one subject.

2. Permission to use wet materials (water-colours, oils, pen and ink, modelling-clay, etc.) must be obtained in advance.

3. *Short-period permits* of up to three days may be obtained either on personal application to the Keeper of the Department concerned, or on written application to the Director. Applicants are required to specify the Galleries in which they wish to work, to state their qualifications and to give their permanent address. The Trustees may also require a written recommendation (see para. 4c below).

4. *Long-period permits,* valid for one year, may be issued on the following conditions:

(*a*) A separate permit is required for each Department.

(*b*) Application should be made in writing to the Director at least three days before the permit is required. Applicants are required to specify the galleries in which they wish to work, to state their qualifications and to give their permanent address.

(*c*) Each application should be accompanied by a letter of recommendation from a person of recognised position based upon personal knowledge of the applicant and certifying that he or she is a fit and proper person to be granted such facilities. In the case of students attending an art school, the letter of recommendation should preferably be written by a member of the teaching staff of the institution concerned. The Trustees cannot accept the recommendations of hotel or boarding-house keepers in favour of their guests.

5. Permits to use wet materials in the exhibition galleries must be produced if required; they are not transferable. Long-period permits may be renewed on written application to the Director.

6. Visitors working with wet materials are urged to exercise the greatest care in their use so that no damage is caused to the collections, cases, mounts, floors, or walls.

7. Permits may at any time be suspended by the Director and they may at any time be withdrawn by the Trustees, or their renewal refused by the Trustees, at their absolute discretion.

HOW TO OBTAIN A TICKET FOR THE USE OF STUDENTS' ROOMS

A number of regulations are in force to safeguard the collections, to make the best use of the limited accommodation in students' rooms, and to ensure that these facilities are freely accessible to all interested persons who are studying a subject related to the collections in the various departments.

READING ROOM PART VIEW

STUDENTS' ROOM OF THE DEPARTMENT OF MANUSCRIPTS

STUDENTS' ROOM OF THE DEPARTMENT OF
ORIENTAL PRINTED BOOKS AND MANUSCRIPTS

By courtesy of the Ministry of Works

THE ROYAL MUSIC LIBRARY

A ticket may be issued on the understanding that the visitor cannot elsewhere obtain the facilities for research and reference.

Short-term tickets for a limited period are normally given on direct application to the Keeper. It is suggested that the visitor bring a letter of introduction from a person of recognised standing, whose address can be identified from the ordinary sources of reference.

Long-term tickets extending up to one year, will be issued after application to the Director, at least two days before the ticket is needed. A letter of introduction based upon personal knowledge of the applicant should be sent with the application.

No charge is made for such tickets.

All ticket holders are required to observe the regulations applicable in each students' room.

The times during which the students' rooms are open can be found in the appropriate section in this book.

For information regarding tickets for the Reading Room see pages 24–5.

No admission ticket is needed for the National Reference Library of Science and Invention.

Department of Printed Books

I. THE COLLECTIONS

THE DEPARTMENT OF Printed Books contains printed material of every type, of all periods from the invention of printing to the present day, and in all languages except those for which the Department of Oriental Printed Books and Manuscripts is responsible. It is the largest library in the United Kingdom and one of the largest in the world.

The department's collections have been steadily built up, since the foundation of the Museum in 1753, by the acquisition of important private collections of books, by systematic purchases, by gifts, and by the operation of the Copyright Acts, which require the deposit in the Museum of a copy of every book, pamphlet or periodical published in the United Kingdom. Publications of Colonial governments are also deposited, and those of foreign governments are obtained through an international exchange system. The total number of volumes in the Department is estimated to be not less than six millions. Additions are at present being made at the rate of well over one million items per annum, made up of 100,000 books and pamphlets, more than 900,000 parts of periodicals and serials and single sheet publications, nearly 200,000 issues of newspapers, about 15,000 maps and 10,000 pieces of music.

The collection of English books is the largest in the world, and efforts are constantly directed at making it as nearly as possible complete. It ranges from Caxtons and the earliest editions of Shakespeare, the English Bible and all the major works of English literature to current newspapers and the latest periodicals. It includes not only the serious and important books and periodicals on every subject, but many thousands of obscure and ephemeral publications of all periods, a large proportion of which are probably preserved in no other library. It may be less well known that the collections in foreign languages are also outstanding and are continually being added to by the acquisition of both current and older works. It can be claimed with confidence that, in a number of European languages, the Department does in fact realise the ideal expressed by a former Principal Librarian that it should be the greatest collection of the literature of each foreign country outside that country itself. Special catalogues of early books have been published, showing holdings of 30,000 German, 21,000 Italian, 12,500 French, 3,000 Spanish and Portuguese, 11,000 Dutch and Belgian books published before 1601.

The collections of the works of individual authors, both English and foreign, are made as complete as possible by the acquisition, when opportunity offers, of editions not previously represented.

Special attention is also given to augmenting and expanding the Museum's collection of fine printing and 'private press' books. Examples of early printed books, often hitherto unknown, are regularly added to the already extensive collection of works issued by fifteenth and sixteenth century printers at home and abroad, and every effort is being made to improve the representation of later presses. For many of these the Museum's collection is nearly complete.

The collection of Russian (pre-revolutionary and Soviet) and East European material is probably the largest in Western Europe, though many of the Museum's Russian and East European literary journals up to 1940 were lost in the bombing of the Second World War and have only been partially replaced.

The acquisition of current material continues, not only from the U.S.S.R. and the countries of Eastern Europe, but also from other countries where émigrés have settled.

It should be noted that literature in Georgian, Armenian and those languages of the U.S.S.R. belonging to the Asian families of languages is kept in the Department of Oriental Printed Books and

Manuscripts and is not entered in the catalogues of the Department of Printed Books.

The department has a fine collection of English and foreign bookbindings. The majority of the best examples come from the Old Royal Library, the King's Library, the Cracherode and Grenville Libraries, the Felix Slade (1868) and Charles Ramsden (1958) bequests and the Henry Davis Gift (1968).[1]

An idea of the scope of the department's resources may be given by listing a few of the most important collections which have been incorporated in it:

1. Sir Hans Sloane's Library, which was one of the foundation collections.

2. The Old Royal Library—the collection formed over several centuries by the Kings and Queens of England and including about 9,000 printed volumes, many specially bound for their royal owners. Transferred to the British Museum in 1757 by George II.

3. The Thomason tracts—a collection of over 20,000 pamphlets relating to the Civil War, Commonwealth and Restoration, made by George Thomason, a contemporary bookseller. Presented by George III. A special catalogue has been published by the Museum.

4. The Cracherode Library—a collection of editions of the classics and finely produced and bound books bequeathed to the Museum in 1799 by the Rev. C. M. Cracherode.

5. David Garrick's collection of English plays. Bequeathed to the Museum.

6. Three large collections of French revolutionary pamphlets, totalling some 80,000 items, obtained from or on the recommendation of John Wilson Croker.

7. The library of Charles Burney (son of the musician), including his collection of newspapers, mainly of the 18th century, in 700

---

[1] Much of the binding of, and repairs to, the Department's collections are carried out in the Museum's bindery, which is under the management of H.M. Stationery Office.

volumes, of which a manuscript catalogue is kept in the Reading Room.

8. The library of Sir Joseph Banks, the 18th century naturalist and President of the Royal Society.

9. The library of King George III, known as the King's Library and housed in the gallery of the same name which was specially built to receive it in 1826. His topographical and maritime collections are now housed in the Map Room.

10. The Grenville Library, bequeathed in 1847 by the Rt. Hon. Thomas Grenville. It contains many early printed books, and is notable for the excellent condition of the volumes.

11. The Tapling collection of postage stamps, bequeathed in 1891, for which a guide has been published by the Museum. This forms the basis of the Department's notable stamp collection, which includes the philatelic archives of Thomas De La Rue and the Stamping Department of the Board of Inland Revenue, the Fitzgerald Airmails, the Mosely African stamps, the Crawford Library of philatelic books and numerous other collections of lesser importance.

12. Edwin Chadwick's collection of pamphlets on economic and social questions, including many from the library of Jeremy Bentham.

13. The Royal Music Library, deposited on permanent loan in 1911 and presented to the Museum by Her Majesty Queen Elizabeth II in 1957. This collection is notable chiefly for its manuscripts, which include many volumes of Handel autographs, but is housed in the Music Room of the Department of Printed Books.

14. The Ashley Library, formed by T. J. Wise, containing original editions of most of the major English poets. Bought in 1937. It is described in Wise's own catalogue which was privately printed.

15. The Paul Hirsch Music Library, a collection of 18,000 items including much rare musical literature, bought in 1946. The

Museum's two special Accession parts, covering the whole collection, were compiled when it was incorporated into the Department's Music and General Catalogues, and are available. Hirsch's own catalogue, of which only four volumes were issued, was never completed.

To this list of collections made outside the Museum and acquired complete must be added one outstanding collection formed and organised within the Department, and constituting a distinct section of the library, the collection of *incunabula*. It comprises nearly 10,400 different editions of works printed up to the end of 1500, a total approached elsewhere only by the Staatsbibliothek at Munich and the Bibliothèque Nationale in Paris. The collection is strong over the whole field of 15th century printing, both in the representation of printers and types from the various countries and towns, and in the variety of authors and texts. Entries for all incunabula in the Museum Library are included in the General Catalogue. Those printed in Germany, Italy, France, Holland and Belgium are also more fully described in the *Catalogue of XVth Century Books now in the British Museum*, parts i–ix (1908–62). The catalogue will be completed by volumes comprising Spain and Portugal (to appear in 1970), England, later acquisitions, and indexes. A photographic reprint of parts i–viii, made from the departmental copy, containing manuscript corrections and additional notes, was published in 1963, and part ix, Holland and Belgium was reprinted in 1967.

2. THE CATALOGUES

All the books in the Department (excluding newspapers, maps, music, certain minor publications and the books in the National Reference Library of Science and Invention), are recorded in the *General Catalogue*. In its published form this consists of 263 volumes containing all books catalogued before the end of 1955, with a ten-year supplement for 1956–65. In the Reading Room itself the

Catalogue takes the form of 1,600 large folio volumes in which columns from the printed Catalogue have been mounted, together with added entries for books acquired more recently. Entries for recent books not yet incorporated in the volumes of the main Catalogue may be found in a card index also kept in the Reading Room.

Entries in the General Catalogue are normally under authors' names, arranged alphabetically. There are also entries under governments, societies and institutions, for their official publications, and for anonymous books under headings taken from their titles. Entries for periodical publications (other than those issued by governments, societies and institutions) will be found under their titles. Readers seeking works on a particular subject are catered for by the Subject Index. In this, nearly all books in the library published since the year 1880 are entered under an alphabetical series of subject headings. The Subject Index has been printed in instalments, each covering a five-year period. The first four instalments covering books acquired from 1881 to 1900 were cumulated. Publication of the Index for 1951–55 has been temporarily delayed, but the series is otherwise complete to 1960. Well over a million distinct publications are recorded in it.

There are separate catalogues for the Newspaper Library, the Map Room, the Music Room and the National Reference Library of Science and Invention. Copies of the newspaper, map and music catalogues are also available in the Reading Room. The basic arrangement of entries in the Newspaper Catalogue is by the place of publication of the newspaper, in the Map Catalogue by the area or place represented, and in the Music Catalogue by names of composers.

Certain special catalogues are noted above in the notes on the collections.

3. ACCESS TO THE COLLECTIONS

1. The book-stacks housing the collections are normally closed to the public and books are seen in the various reading rooms, where they are delivered to readers on application. Books must not be removed from the room in which they are issued. Tickets of admission to the Reading Room* are issued free to persons over the age of 21 requiring facilities for research and reference which are not readily available in the libraries normally accessible to them.

2. For the admission of persons under 21 years of age a special order from the Trustees is necessary.

3. Tickets of admission are issued on the following conditions:

(a) That they are not transferable, and must be produced on demand;

(b) That they may be at any time suspended by the Director; and

(c) That they may be at any time withdrawn by the Trustees, or their renewal refused by the Trustees, at their absolute discretion.

4. Reading Room tickets are of two kinds: Long-period Tickets, valid in the first instance for a period not exceeding one year, and Short-period Tickets, valid for a period not exceeding six days, and not normally issued to those wishing to be regular users of the Reading Room. Long-period Tickets may be renewed if need is shown.

---

* 'Reading Room' is to be understood as the Reading Room and North Library. The regulations for admission, etc., also apply to the State Paper Room, the Map Room and the Newspaper Library Reading Room but the separate paragraphs on each of these should be consulted for other relevant information. Apart from the restriction on the use of Short-Period Tickets, one ticket grants admission to all these reading rooms. No ticket of admission is needed for the National Reference Library of Science and Invention.

5. LONG-PERIOD TICKETS. These are the normal tickets of admission. Application for them should be made in writing to the Director of the British Museum and sent to THE DIRECTOR (READERS' TICKETS), BRITISH MUSEUM, LONDON, W C I; applicants are required to give their full name and permanent address and to state the *specific* purpose for which they seek admission, adding the particulars necessary to show that the use of the Reading Room is required for *research in the sense of paragraph 1.*

The application should be accompanied by a written recommendation from a person of recognised position based upon *personal* knowledge of the applicant and certifying that he or she is a fit and proper person to use the Reading Room. Applications for tickets from students attending a university or other educational institution must be accompanied by a recommendation from a member of the staff of the institution who can certify that the applicant is an advanced student who needs to make use of the resources of the British Museum Library. The Trustees cannot accept the recommendation of hotel or boarding-house keepers in favour of their guests.

6. SHORT-PERIOD TICKETS. These are intended for persons desiring to make only temporary use of the Reading Room and do not of themselves entitle the holder to enter the North Library, which is the rare book room. Application may be made either personally at the Director's Office when admission is required, or in writing to the Director. Applicants are required to state the *specific* purpose for which they seek admission and to give their permanent address. The Trustees may also require a written recommendation as described in paragraph 5.

7. The Reading Room and other rooms are open every week-day including Bank Holidays—*except* Good Friday, Christmas Day, Boxing Day and the week beginning with the first Monday in May.

The hours of opening are—

	Mon., Fri., Sat.	Tues., Wed., Thurs.
Reading Room	9.00 a.m. – 5.00 p.m.	9.00 a.m. – 9.00 p.m.
State Paper Room	9.30 a.m. – 4.45 p.m.	9.30 a.m. – 8.45 p.m.
Map Room	9.30 a.m. – 4.30 p.m.	
Newspaper Library Reading Room	10.00 a.m. – 5.00 p.m.	

8. All communications respecting the use of the Reading Room should be addressed to THE DIRECTOR, BRITISH MUSEUM WCI, and any telephone enquiries made to 01-636 1555, ext. 350.

REGULATIONS FOR THE USE OF THE READING ROOM

The regulations to be observed inside the reading rooms are contained in the pamphlet *British Museum Reading Room Regulations,* which a new reader should study carefully, together with the companion pamphlet entitled *Notes for Readers,* which describes the procedures to be followed in using the Department's facilities. The following paragraphs mention only those few procedures which affect every prospective reader in planning his first visit. Other important information is given in the paragraphs on the various reading rooms.

Application slips must be handed in before 4.15 p.m., or before 8 p.m. on days when the Reading Room is open until 9 p.m. (N.B. Slips for music and maps must be handed in before 4.15 p.m.) The interval between application and delivery is normally from half-an-hour to an hour.

Small numbers of books may also be reserved in advance by postal application. Letters should be addressed to the SUPERINTENDENT OF THE READING ROOM, THE BRITISH MUSEUM, LONDON, W.C.I, and should be posted so that they will reach the Superintendent at least 24 hours before the books are required.

Books put into reserve for a reader will not be kept in reserve during his absence if applied for by another reader present in the Museum. When he arrives, the first reader will have to apply for them again by writing new application slips.

The Museum cannot receive telephone calls, messages or mail on behalf of readers.

FURTHER INFORMATION ON THE VARIOUS ROOMS

The Reading Room

The Reading Room, a large circular room with seats for 390 readers, is the centre of the library and has been in regular use since 1857. In it the catalogues are kept, applications for books are received, and most of the books are read. A classified reference collection of some 30,000 volumes is kept in the Reading Room on open shelves. Other books are obtained by writing particulars taken from the General Catalogue on printed application slips, and books are delivered to the reader's seat. Special staff are on continuous duty in the Enquiry Desk in the Reading Room to help readers to use the library and to direct them to sources of information on the subjects they are studying.

Readers may use their own typewriters in the typing room on the East side of the passage between the Reading Room and the North Library.

The Periodicals Gallery

Current parts of some much used periodicals are on open shelves in the Periodicals Gallery, which is reached from the corridor to the left of the entrance to the North Library. It is also used as a Reading Room for all unbound parts and for large or bulky material. Microfilm and microprint readers are situated on the gallery.

The North Library

The North Library, access to which is through the main Reading

Room, is reserved for the reading of early and rare books and other material requiring special care or supervision. It has seats for 120 readers and a limited number of shelves which are allocated for periods up to six months to persons engaged on prolonged research requiring the simultaneous use of many volumes. Reference books of particular use to readers using early and rare books are kept on open shelves in this room.

A collating machine is available to aid in detecting variant readings in different copies of the same edition.

Special Divisions

1. *The State Paper Room*

The State Paper Room is a division of the Library devoted to government publications. It contains a small separate Reading Room, which provides a reference service for readers working in this field.

The State Paper Room makes available to the public a comprehensive collection of government publications from all parts of the world. Open access is given to a set of British Parliamentary Papers (which includes the scarce 111 volume Abbot Collection[1]) and also to Public, Local and Private Acts, Parliamentary Debates and other primary sources. The latest issues of the United Kingdom Registers of Voters are also available for consultation. Among foreign government publications are included (by arrangement with the Department of Oriental Printed Books and Manuscripts) many in oriental languages.

In maintaining the collection the State Paper Room is able to make use of the system of international exchanges of official publications conducted by the Stationery Office. It is also a depository for all Colonial official publications, and for publications of the United Nations and other international organisations.

---

[1] The Abbot Collection is a set of 18th century Parliamentary papers collected by the Speaker, Charles Abbot. Four sets only were made (1804–1807) of which the Museum has the only complete set accessible to the public.

The aim of this division of the Department of Printed Books is to bring together all the main printed sources of primary character for the study of public administration of all periods, as well as the more important publications of government research organisations.

Readers requiring government publications may read them in either the main Reading Room or the State Paper Room by application on the usual slips. As many government publications are not in the Catalogue, those who cannot find there the titles they need, or have difficulty in identifying their reference, are advised to consult the State Paper Room directly.

2. The Map Room

The Map Room houses the Museum's main collection of printed maps and atlases. A comprehensive series of early maps and atlases, dating from the 15th century, serves the needs of historical research; of particular importance are King George the Third's Topographical and Maritime Collections, comprising some 50,000 maps and charts which formed the finest geographical collection of its day, and the Crace Collection of London plans. A complete set of British Ordnance Survey maps is preserved, beginning with the original manuscript surveys (1791–1824) for the first edition of the one inch to one mile map of England and Wales. In the field of contemporary map production the Map Room acquires all material published in the British Isles, and up-to-date topographical coverage of other countries in medium and small scales, together with a representative collection of general and thematic maps and atlases.

The Catalogue of Printed Maps is a geographical index, arranged in alphabetical order, in which maps, atlases, plans and views are entered under the name of the place, region, or feature represented. Added entries are made under the names of cartographers and engravers. A new (photolithographic) edition of the *Catalogue of Printed Maps, Charts and Plans* published in 15 volumes in 1967, records the holdings of the Museum up to the end of 1964. A card catalogue containing entries for later accessions is maintained in the Map Room and will be published at intervals of five years as a Supplement to the Map Catalogue.

A Students' Room is provided with an open-access reference library. Readers are admitted to the Room on the production of a Readers' Ticket or a letter from the Superintendent. Application for maps may be made either in the Map Room or in the main Reading Room, where a copy of the Map Catalogue up to 1964 is provided, and special application forms are supplied. Although maps of convenient size may be consulted in the North Library, a reader requiring more than a limited number of maps should consult them in the Map Room. Readers wishing to study the large-scale plans of the Ordnance Survey are requested to give 24 hours' notice to the Map Room. The supply of sheet maps of parts of the world outside Europe may also be subject to some delay.

The Map Room maintains an information service, and also executes photographic orders. It has a collection of 35 mm. colour slides, of which duplicates are available for purchase. Facsimiles on sale include the county maps of England and Wales by Christopher Saxton, 1584–79, and Baptista Boazio's map of Ireland, c. 1599.

3. The Music Room

The scope of the Music Room covers printed music of all periods, including methods and tutors and early works of musical theory. Here, as in the rest of the Library, a large and representative collection of older material both British and foreign is combined with a very complete accumulation of modern British publications of every kind received by deposit under the Copyright Act of 1911. Current foreign music is also well represented. At present the collection contains about one and a quarter million pieces of music.

The Royal Music Library (consisting partly of manuscripts) is kept in the Music Room, as is also the whole of the Paul Hirsch

Music Library, which, in addition to scores, includes a large number of works about music.

All printed music in the collections, including that in the Royal Music Library, is normally made available in the Reading Room. Application slips must be handed in in the Reading Room or North Library not later than 4.15 p.m. Manuscripts in the Royal Music Library (shelfmarks R.M. 18–R.M. 24), the use of which is covered by special regulations, may be consulted only in the Music Room itself. Readers may also be admitted to the Music Room:

(a) when they require a large quantity of music in a short time,
(b) when they need to consult the classified card catalogues and the typed index to uncatalogued secondary vocal music (1890 to date), neither of which is available in the Reading Room,
(c) when they require advice or information which the Enquiry Desk of the Reading Room cannot supply.

The staff of the Music Room provides, in answer to enquiries, information about musical sources required for research or performance; about musical literature and bibliography, and about various aspects of music librarianship. The Music Room is open from 9.30 a.m. to 4.30 p.m. from Monday to Friday, and from 9.30 a.m. to 1 p.m. on Saturday.

The British Museum does not collect gramophone records (enquiries should be addressed to the British Institute of Recorded Sound, 29 Exhibition Road, S.W.7.), nor has it a collection of musical instruments. Music manuscripts, other than those contained in the Royal Music Library, are kept in the Department of Manuscripts.

Visitors who wish to study printed or manuscript music in the collections of the British Museum should apply to the Director's Office for a ticket of admission to the Library or to the Manuscript Department.

4. *The Newspaper Library*

Newspapers are housed in the British Museum Newspaper Library, Colindale Avenue, London, N.W.9, opposite Colindale

Tube Station, on the Northern line. It contains all the newspapers held by the Department of Printed Books (with the exception of London newspapers issued before 1801, which are kept in the main building at Bloomsbury[1]) and most of the weekly periodicals. All modern English newspapers, virtually complete apart from gaps caused by bomb damage, are included, as well as a good selection of newspapers of the Commonwealth and of foreign countries. There is a Reading Room accommodating 48 readers, to which admission is obtained by tickets issued on the same conditions as those for the Reading Room at Bloomsbury, which are themselves also valid at Colindale. The Newspaper Library also contains an extensive installation for making microfilms. A number of important current newspapers are recorded regularly on microfilm, and microfilm copies of newspapers in the collection can be supplied, subject to conditions of copyright.

The Reading Room is open daily—except Sundays, Good Friday, Christmas Day, Boxing Day, and the week beginning with the first Monday in May. The hours are from ten o'clock in the morning until five o'clock in the evening throughout the year.

4. OTHER SERVICES

1. *Information Service*

For many years it has been part of the duty of the Reading Room staff to help readers to find the information they require. From this, not unnaturally, there has developed a considerable postal service. This deals in the first place with bibliographical queries about books recorded in the library's catalogues, and with the question whether or not a particular piece of printed matter is to

---

[1] The *London, Edinburgh, Belfast and Dublin Gazettes* are also kept at Bloomsbury. Additional files of *The Times* (1809 to date), *The Times Literary Supplement*, and the *Illustrated London News* (1844–92) are also kept at Bloomsbury.

Readers are warned that some provincial newspapers have been lost as a result of enemy action and that storage conditions may make it necessary to restrict the supply of certain classes of newspapers from time to time.

THE MAP READING ROOM

THE STATE PAPER ROOM

THE ARCH ROOM HOUSING INCUNABULA

be found in the collections. Information is given on the location of books not held by the Museum, when this can be obtained from published sources: in other cases the question may be referred to the National Central Library. In addition, enquiries on a vast range of topics are received, and, whenever possible, informative answers are given—usually in the form of references to books and articles for the enquirer to consult. When some institution is known to specialise in a subject covering the enquiry, the letter may be forwarded to that institution. The enquirer will then be informed.

2. *Photography*

Photographic copies, including microfilms, from publications in the collections can be obtained, subject to the provisions of the Copyright Acts and related regulations, and provided there is no risk of damage to fragile items. The photography itself and the administrative work connected with it are the responsibility of the British Museum Photographic Service, but help is given by the staff of the Department in identifying the matter to be photographed and in solving copyright problems in relation to it. Orders for photographs can be handed in to the Director's Office or sent by post to the Photographic Service, British Museum, W.C.1. A Xerox Rapid Copy service is available in the various reading rooms and is described on pages 13–15.

5. **EXHIBITIONS**

The King's Library, a handsome gallery 300 feet long, which was built for, and still contains, the library collected by George III, is the oldest part of the present Museum building. It serves as an exhibition gallery for the Departments of Printed Books and Oriental Printed Books and Manuscripts. In it is displayed a permanent exhibition illustrating the history of printing, and ranging from 15th-century block-books and the Gutenberg bibles to examples of fine printing of the present century. Bindings, notable recent acquisitions, and first editions of famous English books are also regularly exhibited. These exhibits are supplemented and at times replaced by temporary exhibitions of books, often illustrating a subject of topical interest.

At the north end of the gallery will be found the Tapling Collection of postage and telegraph stamps of the world (1840–90), the Mosely Collection of stamps of British Africa (1847–1935), the Fitzgerald Collection of Airmail stamps and souvenirs, the Bojanowicz Collection of Poland, (1939–47) and selections of material from the Universal Postal Union and Inland Revenue stamp collections.

There is a small exhibition space at the North Entrance to the Museum which is used for the display of maps and globes.

THE NATIONAL REFERENCE LIBRARY OF SCIENCE AND INVENTION

This Library houses that part of the Museum's collection of modern scientific and technical literature considered to be of value to current research and development.

All the literature is freely available for consultation by the public. No reader's ticket or prior appointment is necessary. The N.R.L.S.I. does not lend its literature, so that its holdings are always available for consultation. Moreover, subject to the usual requirements of the Copyright Act, photocopies—at ninepence per page—can be supplied immediately to personal callers, or quickly by post in response to telex or postal requests.

At present the Library is organised in two parts, known as the Holborn and Bayswater Divisions.

THE HOLBORN DIVISION

The Holborn Division is situated at 25 Southampton Buildings, Chancery Lane, London, W.C.2., where it shares a common entrance with the Patent Office. Southampton Buildings is a street linking High Holborn and Chancery Lane. Bus routes 7, 8, 22, 23 and 25 run from near the British Museum (v.s.) to High Holborn (Gray's Inn Road stop). The library is open from 9.30 a.m. to 9 p.m. Monday to Friday and from 10 a.m. to 1 p.m. on Saturday. However the Foreign patents annexe is open only from 9.30 a.m. to 5.30 p.m. Monday to Friday and is closed on Saturday. The Library is closed on public holidays.

Since 1855 (when it was founded as the Patent Office Library) the Holborn Division has been devoted to the service of those concerned with invention and technological progress. In consequence it now contains nearly half a million bound volumes of scientific and technical periodicals and books, and includes a complete holding of British patents publications and the only comprehensive set of foreign patents publications in this country. Its literature is mainly that of the physical sciences (mathematics, chemistry, physics, etc.), engineering and industrial technologies and skills. There are also substantial holdings of material dealing with other fields of knowledge which have a bearing on developments in the main subject areas.

Most of the works held by the Holborn Division are on open shelves to which readers have direct access. Requests for material in store should be made before 4.45 p.m., Monday to Friday, at the Central Information Desk, or by telephone.

Layout

A cloakroom is provided in the vestibule where visitors should leave bags and cases (except ladies' handbags), since these may not be taken into the library. Visitors are required to sign the Visitors' Register once each day before using the library. The vestibule houses public telephones and also personal lockers which may be hired by library users for a nominal quarterly rental.

The main library is on four levels, and there is an annexe in a nearby building. Maps showing the arrangement of the library are to be found in the vestibule, on the ground floor by the Central Information Desk and at each of the other levels.

The Literature Collections

The literature in the Holborn Division is divided into eight main collections:

Collections	*Location*
1. Books	Ground floor, far end
2. Pamphlets	On bottom shelf below books
3. Abstracting periodicals	Lower ground floor
4. Other periodicals, unbound issues	Ground and Lower ground floors
5. Other periodicals, bound volumes	First and second galleries
6. Trade literature	Ground floor, near Centre Desk
7. British patents literature	Ground floor, vestibule end
8. Overseas patents literature	Library annexe, Chancery House, lower ground floor

Within each of the book, pamphlet and periodical collections the literature is arranged on the shelves in order of its subject matter. The individual subjects are distinguished by means of the classmarks used in the Library's own classification scheme; these most commonly comprise two capital letters followed by two figures (e.g. AK 21).

To find literature by subject, it is necessary to use the Classified Catalogue and its Index, both of which are near the Central Information Desk. Likewise, to locate a known reference it is necessary to use the Author and Name Catalogue or one of the other indexes.

Trade literature is arranged in alphabetical order by the manufacturer's name. Items are not catalogued individually, but there is an entry in the Author and Name Catalogue, on a green card, for each company represented.

British patent specifications are arranged in numerical order in the full height stacks. Most of the other items, which are aids to searching among patent specifications, are contained in or on the half-height stacks in the centre of the area. They include:

Abridgments (summaries of patents in subject groups or classes)
Key to the Classification of Patents for Invention
   (the classification used for patent specifications is quite different from that
   used for technical books and periodicals)
Reference Index to the Classification of Patents
Name index to published specifications
Name index to recent applicants (current and last six years)
Applications Register
Register of Stages of Progress
Official Journal (Patents)
Trade Marks Journal

Foreign patents literature, located in the annexe in nearby Chancery House, is arranged in alphabetical order of the issuing country. Generally the material for each country comprises firstly the official gazette (if one is issued) and then the patent specifications in numerical order. Name and subject searches can usually be made by means of the indexes which are issued either separately or as part of the official journals. Other aids may also be of value in particular instances.

Material of earlier date is shelved in a reserve area of the annexe but can be obtained for use in the public area upon application to the enquiry desk. A comprehensive set of foreign language technical dictionaries and glossaries largely duplicating those in the other reading rooms is available in the annexe. Although the annexe closes at 5.30 p.m. and is not open on Saturday, foreign patents literature can be made available in the main library in the evenings and on Saturday by prior arrangement.

A cloakroom is situated at the entrance to the annexe. Visitors should leave bags and cases there (except ladies' handbags) since these may not be taken into the foreign patents area. Visitors are also required to sign the Register, which is at the cloakroom desk, once each day before using the annexe.

Catalogues and Indexes
To help readers to find what they require among the Holborn

Division's stock, several card catalogues and indexes are provided; they include:

Author and Name Catalogue
Classified Subject Catalogue
Index to the Classified Catalogue (Subject Index)
Periodicals Index
Bibliographies Index
Translations Index
Dictionaries Catalogue

A version of the Author and Name catalogue of the Bayswater Division stock is maintained at Holborn, situated opposite the Central Information Desk on the ground floor of the main library.

THE BAYSWATER DIVISION

The Bayswater Division is situated at 10 Porchester Gardens, London, W.2, off Queensway. The nearest Underground station is Bayswater, while Queensway may be used for travelling via the Central Line from Chancery Lane station and the Holborn Division. Bus routes 12 and 88 (Bayswater Road) and 7, 15, 27 and 36 (Westbourne Grove) pass near the Bayswater Division.

The reading room of the Bayswater Division is open from 9.30 a.m. until 5.30 p.m., Monday to Friday. It is closed on public holidays.

Broadly speaking, the Bayswater Division holds all the literature of the natural sciences and technologies not held at the Holborn Division. In consequence it is particularly strong in the literature of the basic life sciences (botany, zoology, etc.) and their applications, and in the literature of the less familiar languages.

Because its building is unsuitable for an open-access library, most of the stock is in reserve stores. The reading room, however, contains for immediate consultation on open shelves the more important abstracting journals and other source material which the Division holds, together with a substantial collection of dictionaries and other reference tools.

To obtain a work from reserve store, a request form should be completed with the appropriate details taken from the catalogue and then handed to the staff desk. The work will normally be brought to the reading room within a few minutes. Requests should be made by 5.00 p.m.

Layout

Access to the reading room is through the Porchester Gardens entrance to the Division, and then by lift to the first floor.

A cloakroom is provided where readers should leave bags and cases (except ladies' handbags), since these may not be taken into the reading room. Visitors are also required to sign the Visitors' Register once each day before using the reading room.

Catalogues and Indexes

An Author and Name catalogue of the Bayswater stock is provided. There is also an index to periodicals and a subject catalogue which lists works in the order of the new N.R.L.S.I. subject classification—which is essentially a radically modernised and expanded form of the classification still in use at the Holborn Division.

Publications

To promote the use of the important periodical literature held by the N.R.L.S.I. lists are published giving details of the titles currently received in each Division.

For the Holborn Division the latest available edition (which still carries the Library's former title) is *Periodical Publications in the Patent Office Library. List of Current Titles.* 3rd edition 1965. Price 28s. 0d. from H.M.S.O. (29s. 9d. post free). A new edition is due to be published in summer 1970.

For the Bayswater Division *Periodical Publications in the National Reference Library of Science and Invention, Part I. List of non-Slavonic titles in the Bayswater Division* 1969, published by the British Museum, price 25s. 0d, is available.

OTHER PUBLIC SERVICES

The N.R.L.S.I. runs introductory courses to familiarise readers with the resources provided. It also collaborates with other bodies running courses on the organisation or exploitation of technical literature by arranging guided tours of the Library.

An enquiry service is provided to help those unable to visit the Library to draw upon its resources. Requests for short bibliographies or items of specific information can be accepted, but the amount of time that can be devoted to each enquiry is limited.

The N.R.L.S.I. also issues a number of descriptive guides to its services and definitive bibliographies of selected portions of its literature resources, under the series titles *Aids to Readers*. These are free of charge and copies and further details are obtainable upon application to the Library.

THE STUDENTS' ROOM IN THE DEPARTMENT OF PRINTS AND DRAWINGS

THE HOLBORN DIVISION OF THE NATIONAL REFERENCE
LIBRARY OF SCIENCE AND INVENTION, A PART
OF THE BRITISH MUSEUM

Department of Manuscripts

Office: Entrance in the Manuscript Saloon

THE PRINCIPAL SERVICE to the public provided by the Department of Manuscripts is the Manuscript Students' Room.

The entrance to the Students' Room is from the Manuscript Saloon. Entry is by ticket of admission only, and tickets must be shown to the warder on duty on each occasion of entering the Students' Room. Applications for tickets must be made to the Director's Office on the printed form supplied.

The Students' Room possesses accommodation for approximately sixty students. Any seat not already occupied may be taken, except that for the study of illuminated manuscripts special places are set aside. Applications for manuscripts are made on printed forms, supplies of which are available in various parts of the room, and the manuscripts are delivered to the student's place. They must be returned to the counter when finished with, or when the room closes; manuscripts can be kept out from day to day if required. Manuscripts can also be ordered in advance by writing direct to the Superintendent of the Students' Room, giving sufficient notice to take account of postal delays. If printed books are required for comparison with manuscripts, application should be made to the Superintendent of the Reading Room, who will arrange for the books to be sent round to the Manuscript Students' Room. Such applications should be made 24 hours in advance.

Round the walls of the room are sets (in duplicate) of the various Departmental catalogues, together with a selection of essential works of reference, catalogues of other manuscript collections, and manuscript facsimiles. For a detailed list of the catalogues of the Department see the official booklet *The Catalogues of the Manuscript Collections* (revised edition 1962).

Two microfilm readers and an ultra-violet lamp for the examination of faded writings are available.

The Department of Manuscripts is the national collection of manuscripts. Its collections comprise books and documents of all kinds written by hand, in all European languages, and ranging in date from Greek papyri of the 3rd century B.C. down to documents of the present day. In addition, manuscript music and manuscript maps, plans and topographical drawings fall within the ambit of the Department. Materials in book form amount to some 70,000 volumes and each volume may contain several hundred separate documents. In addition, there are some 100,000 charters and rolls. The separate categories of material in the Departments are:

1. Manuscripts.
2. Charters and Rolls.
3. Detached seals (including seal impressions, bullae, impressions from seal-matrices, and casts).
4. Papyri and ostraca.
5. Manuscript facsimiles.
6. Microfilms.

A representative selection of material in the Department is on permanent exhibition in the Grenville Library, the Manuscript Saloon, the Bible Room and the Magna Carta Room. A series of temporary exhibitions, devoted to particular subjects and intended to display items not included in the permanent exhibition, is maintained in the two cases nearest to the Front Hall entrance to the Grenville Library. A selection of recent acquisitions is also normally on exhibition.

Subject to a very few restrictions, for which see the detailed regulations, all items in the collections which have been catalogued are freely available to students, and there are in general no restrictions either on the number of manuscripts which may be consulted or (so far as the Museum is concerned) on the use which may be made of their contents.

All photography of items in the collections must be undertaken by the Official Photographer (see pp. 11–13) and applications for photographs, photocopies, microfilms, etc., can be made in the Students' Room. A large stock of negatives is held in the Department, and prints from these can be ordered. Albums containing specimen prints from these negatives are on the shelves of the Students' Room, together with a card index of the manuscripts so photographed. 35 mm. colour transparencies can be made by the Official Photographer, and orders for these can similarly be placed in the Students' Room. Master copies of a large number of 35 mm. colour transparencies are also held in the Department and these can be seen in the Students' Room on application at the counter.

DEPARTMENT OF MANUSCRIPTS

Students' Room

The Students' Room is open on week-days, including Saturdays and Bank Holidays, except for Good Friday, Christmas Day, Boxing Day, and the last complete week in October. The hours are from 10 a.m. until 4.45 p.m. throughout the year.

Department of Oriental Printed Books and Manuscripts

Scope of the Collections

THE RANGE OF languages and cultures covered by the books and manuscripts in this Department is very wide. Briefly, it extends from Morocco in the west, through North Africa, the Near and Middle East, the whole of Asia (excluding Russia but including the Indian Sub-continent and South-east Asia), to China and Japan in the east. The languages concerned fall into certain well-defined groups, each under the charge of language specialists. (1) Hebrew, Syriac, Aramaic. (2) Arabic. (3) Turkish, Persian, Pushtu and the language of Soviet Central Asia. (4) Sanskrit and other languages of north India. (5) Dravidian languages of south India. (6) The languages of South-east Asia. (7) Chinese, Korean, Mongol. (8) Japanese.

Altogether, the collections number some 35,000 manuscripts and 250,000 printed books. The numbers are constantly increasing through purchase, donation and exchange. In the course of time the Museum has acquired large numbers of oriental manuscripts of intrinsic worth and beauty, as well as early printed books of antiquarian interest, but the collections in the Department are by no means confined to such rarities. They also constitute a working library for the orientalist, who needs the reference tools of modern scholarship, and for the student anxious to learn more about the civilisations of the East. It is the policy of the Department, as a part of the National Library, to build up a representative collection of books of scholarly value in all the languages of the oriental world, and to make them available to readers. Only books and manuscripts written in oriental languages, or translated from them, will be found in this Department. All works in western languages, except essential reference works which are available to readers on the open shelves in the Students' Room, are placed in the Department of Printed Books and may be consulted in the Reading Room of that Department. Books are freely interchangeable between the two Reading Rooms on occasions when a reader needs to consult two texts side by side, one western and one oriental, for purposes of comparison.

The Catalogues

The collections are catalogued primarily by language. In many of the languages covered by the Department printed catalogues have already been published, and supplements to these catalogues are issued from time to time. In other languages of smaller scope, where the output of new publications is not so great, there may be as yet no printed catalogue in book form, but provisional handwritten catalogues exist in the Department and may be consulted by any interested readers. Current accessions of printed books in the major oriental languages are catalogued on cards which are placed in the Oriental Students' Room for the use of readers. Manuscript accessions are recorded in a register available in the same room; this has an index volume in which the manuscripts are classified by language for easy reference.

Oriental Students' Room

This is the hub of the Department. It provides comfortable seating for some thirty readers, and is a lofty and spacious room with good natural lighting. Readers wishing to consult oriental books or manuscripts fill in the appropriate tickets and hand them to the officer-in-charge, who will ensure that the books are brought to the reader as quickly as possible. It generally takes less than ten minutes to supply a book or manuscript.

In the Students' Room is a selection of the most important dictionaries, grammars, bibliographies and other reference works having a bearing on oriental studies. All the published catalogues of books and manuscripts in the Department are also available for consultation on the reference shelves.

Readers' Tickets

Long-term readers' tickets will be issued to serious students whose needs cannot be readily satisfied in other libraries open to them. For periods up to one week, however, short-term tickets can be issued to applicants in the Oriental Students' Room by the officer-in-charge there. No ticket of admission to the Students' Room is required for those members of the public who desire information or who bring in books or manuscripts to be identified.

Photographic Services

In common with other Departments of the British Museum, this Department can supply photographic copies of any of its material, sometimes by taking prints from existing negatives, sometimes by photographing a book or manuscript afresh. Prints, photostats, microfilms and colour transparencies can all be supplied, through the Official Photographic Service of the Museum. Application forms for photography may be obtained from the Oriental Students' Room.

A Rapid-copy service is also available, whereby Xerographic copies can be supplied within 24 hours, subject to the normal conditions of the copyright regulations. This applies to printed books and manuscripts, whose condition is judged suitable for photocopying.

A microfilm reader is provided in the Oriental Students' Room for the use of readers who wish to consult microfilms from the departmental collections, or by special permission, microfilms which they themselves possess.

Information Service

The specialist staff of the Department are ready to give information to members of the public on books or manuscripts in the departmental collections, on oriental literature in general, and on books brought in for expert identification (but *not* for valuation). Such enquiries may be made in person, through the officer-in-charge of the Oriental Students' Room, or in writing by addressing a letter to the Keeper of the Department. It is regretted that extensive translation from oriental languages cannot be undertaken by members of the staff.

DEPARTMENT OF ORIENTAL PRINTED BOOKS AND MANUSCRIPTS

Students' Room

The collections of the Department consist chiefly of books and manuscripts written *in oriental languages*, all of which are available for consultation in the Students' Room.

The room is open every week-day, including Bank Holidays—*except* Good Friday, Christmas Day, Boxing Day and the third week of October. The hours of opening are from 10 a.m. to 5 p.m., Monday to Friday, and from 10 a.m. to 1 p.m. on Saturdays.

Department of Prints and Drawings

Students' Room and Exhibition Gallery:
Upper Floor, King Edward VII Gallery

THE DEPARTMENT OF Prints and Drawings, or 'The Print Room' houses the national collection of drawings by Old Masters, of British drawings, and of prints. Its nucleus was formed by several bequests of whole collections of drawings, notably those of Sir Hans Sloane in 1753 and Richard Payne Knight in 1824; to these have been added a continuous series of gifts, bequests and purchases (the most important accessions being the purchase of the Malcolm Collection in 1895, the anonymous gift of the Phillipps-Fenwick Collection in 1946, the Campbell Dodgson Bequest in 1949, as a result of which the British Museum collection, though small by comparison with the great historical Continental accumulations such as the Louvre or the Uffizi, is nonetheless their equal in quality, a notable feature being the outstanding representation of almost every great European artist whose drawings have survived. The collection of British drawings (in which must be counted the Turner Bequest of about 20,000 drawings) and the Césus de Itansee Bequest in 1968, is the largest and most representative in the world. The collection of 'original' prints (e.g. Dürer, Rembrandt, Goya, etc.) is also among the most important, both for its completeness and for the fine quality of its examples. The Department possesses in addition a large number of reproductive prints, as well as others arranged under specialised subject headings.

Italian Drawings

The Department is rich in early drawings, the catalogue of 14th and 15th century works comprising over 350 items. These include the Jacopo Bellini Sketchbook, nine drawings by Giovanni Bellini, three by Botticelli, twenty by Leonardo, and six by Mantegna.

THE STUDENTS' ROOM IN THE DEPARTMENT OF
COINS AND MEDALS

THE STUDENTS' ROOM IN THE DEPARTMENT OF
EGYPTIAN ANTIQUITIES

THE STUDENTS' ROOM IN THE DEPARTMENT OF
WESTERN ASIATIC ANTIQUITIES

The great figures of the 16th century (with the exception of Titian by whom there is only one certain drawing) are well, in some cases superbly, represented, there being eighteen drawings by Correggio, forty by Raphael, and no fewer than eighty-five by Michelangelo. In addition, almost all the more interesting artists of the period are represented by excellent examples.

The 17th and 18th centuries are more sparsely covered, but there are fine drawings by Bernini, Pietro da Cortona, Canaletto, Guardi, Piranesi and the two Tiepolos, to mention only a few of the better known names.

Dutch and Flemish Drawings

The Department has a large share of the few surviving Netherlandish drawings of the 15th century (including two by Rogier van der Weyden), while among the very representative holding of 16th century drawings are eleven by Lucas van Leyden, the largest collection in existence. The 17th century drawings include not only good examples of the work of most of the small masters but outstanding and well balanced groups by the three greatest artists of the period, Rubens, Rembrandt and Van Dyck. There is also an interesting group of water colours of the 18th century Dutch school.

German and Swiss Drawings

Though the German and Swiss schools cannot claim to be as completely represented as either the Italian or the Netherlandish, the Department possesses a number of important 15th century drawings which include examples by Schongauer. In the 16th century, Dürer and the younger Holbein are particularly well represented, the former by well over 100 drawings, the latter by nearly 200, mainly designs for jewellery and ornament. Of later artists, Elsheimer is particularly well represented.

French Drawings

Though this school as a whole is somewhat unevenly represented, particularly for the 19th and 20th centuries, it includes an unrivalled collection of drawings by Claude Lorrain consisting of 323 separately mounted items and a further 200 bound up in the 'Liber Veritatis', formerly at Chatsworth. The collection of sixty-three drawings by Watteau is probably the equal in quality of that at the Louvre. Recent accessions, in particular the de Hauke Bequest, have notably strengthened the 19th century collection which includes fine examples of the work of Prud'hon, Ingres, Géricault, Delacroix, Daumier, Degas, Renoir, Seurat, Toulouse-Lautrec and Odilon Redon.

Spanish Drawings

The Spanish school is represented by a small though not unimportant collection. Of 17th century masters there are good examples of the work of Ribera, Herrera, Murillo, Carreño and Cano. The 18th and 19th centuries are meagrely represented except for Goya, the small group of drawings by whom includes several of the finest quality.

British Drawings

The collection of British drawings is the richest in existence, and covers a period from the 16th century to the present day. At the outset come the famous group of drawings of North American Indians and the *flora* and *fauna* of Raleigh's Virginia by John White, and from the 17th century there are portrait drawings by Lely and his contemporaries and landscape and topographical works by Hollar and his Anglo-Netherlandish successors. Of 18th century figure-artists, Thornhill, Hogarth and Gainsborough are well represented, while the development of English water-colour landscape can be studied in fine examples of William Taverner, Paul Sandby, Alexander and J. R. Cozens, Towne, Girtin, Cotman, Constable, de Wint and Turner. The Department also possesses a good representation of William Blake, not only in his drawings but also in his engraved books and single prints, as well as a small but choice group of drawings by the Pre-Raphaelites.

Prints

Some outstanding features of the collection of original prints are: 15th and 16th century Italian engravings; 15th century German engravings; engravings and woodcuts by Dürer and Lucas van Leyden; 17th century Dutch and Flemish etchings, in which such important artists as Hercules Seghers, Rembrandt and Van Dyck are especially well represented; etchings by Callot; engravings by Hogarth; etchings and lithographs by Goya; English mezzotints. The reference material in the Department includes a large section of prints after masters, so classified under the respective schools, as well as engraved portraits, and topographical, historical, and satirical prints. There are also specialised collections, including playing-cards, fans and fan-leaves, book-plates and trade-cards.

Services

The Students' Room is open to all those in possession of a valid Student's Ticket. Facilities available, in addition to that of consulting the collection itself, include the use of the departmental reference library and the very complete card-index of periodical art-literature, as well as access to a useful collection of photographic and other reproductions of drawings. It must be emphasised, however, that while every assistance is given to the visitor and all facilities for research freely made available, research must be undertaken in person. The staff of the Department answer, to the best of their ability, any questions put to them concerning the authorship and or age of a print or drawing, but they are not permitted to give any information as to its value.

The Exhibition Gallery is open at the same times as the other public galleries of the Museum. In it are held temporary exhibitions of material from the Departmental collection, usually illustrating a particular theme, together with a small display of recent acquisitions.

Print Room

The Print Room is open to students every day in the year, except Sundays, Good Friday, Christmas Day, Boxing Day and such other days as may be appointed. The hours are from 10 a.m. to 1 p.m., 2.15 p.m. to 4 p.m., Monday to Friday, 10 a.m. to 12.30 p.m. Saturday.

Detailed catalogues exist of the following subjects: British Drawings; Drawings from the Turner Bequest; Dutch and Flemish Drawings; Italian Drawings of XIV *c.* and XV *c.*; Drawings by Michelangelo, and Raphael and his School of Parma XVI *c.* Early Italian Engravings; Early German and Flemish Prints; German and Flemish XV *c.* and XVI *c.* Woodcuts; Playing Cards; Fans; Engraved British Portraits; Personal and Political Satires.

Department of Coins and Medals

THE VERY EXTENSIVE National Collection of Coins and Medals had for its nucleus the numismatic cabinets of Sir Robert Cotton (1571–1631) and Sir Hans Sloane (1660–1753), and thus date back to the foundation of the British Museum in 1753. Amongst the outstanding early bequests were the collection of (*a*) the Rev. C. M. Cracherode (1799); (*b*) Miss Sarah Banks and her sister-in-law Dorothea, Lady Banks (1818); (*c*) R. Payne Knight (1824); and the royal collection of coins and medals presented to the nation by King George IV in 1823.

Numerous other important acquisitions have enriched the Department up to the present day. In the *Greek Series* we have such benefactors as James Woodhouse of Corfu (1866); E. P. Thompson, who presented (1922) the magnificent Ashburnham decadrachm of Syracuse; R. B. Seager, whose bequest (1925) enlarged especially the Cretan collection; and Mrs. A. H. Lloyd (1946), whose presentation of the superb collection of the coins of Western Greece amassed by her husband, Dr. A. H. Lloyd, and their daughter, Miss Muriel Lloyd, has been the finest acquisition by the Medal Room in recent years.

In the *Roman Series* the Cracherode coins (1799) and the 'large brass' coins that came to the Museum with the Townley collection in 1814, are among the earliest acquisitions of note. In 1861 the series was enormously enlarged and increased in scientific value by Count John F. W. de Salis, who presented his large collection of Roman money and arranged the Museum series in chronological order. In 1864 Mr. Edward Wigan presented his fine cabinet of Roman gold coins, and in 1866 the purchase of the cabinet of the Duc de Blacas added more than 4,000 coins, many of which are of gold, to the same part of the collection. The 'large brass' coins of the Wigan cabinet (purchased in 1872) are remarkable for their brilliant 'patina' and for uniform excellence of condition. Two important hoards of gold imperial coins from Corbridge were acquired in 1912.

Special note should be made also of the generous donations that have been made through the National Art-Collections Fund during the sixty years of its existence. It is also a pleasure to record the munificent gifts of the Worshipful Company of Goldsmiths at various times, such as two fine collections of gold coins, mainly English and Anglo-Gallic in 1920 and 1922.

English Series

Anglo-Saxon and Early English coins were contained in the Cotton Collection, and the series of English silver pennies was further increased by a purchase from the Rev. Richard Southgate (d. 1795). In 1802 the Museum purchased a series of ancient British and Saxon coins collected by Samuel Tyssen, whose 17th century tokens also eventually found their way into the National Collection. In 1810 the English coins of Barré Charles Roberts were bought for 4,000 guineas. The greater part of the English coins from the cabinet of Sir John Evans was purchased in 1915; in 1919 Sir Arthur Evans presented the collection of Early British and other Celtic coins which had been formed by his father, and Mr. T. H. B. Graham his collection of English silver and copper. Many important and valuable coins have also been acquired from other celebrated cabinets, such as those of Trattle, Shepherd, Montagu and Lockett which, in the course of years, have been offered for sale by auction. Selections from many hoards of Treasure Trove have also materially increased the English series, among which may be instanced the Cuerdale Find of 1840, and the Chancton Find (1866) of coins of Edward the Confessor.

The series of English Medals was largely increased by the purchase in 1860 of the splendid collection (4,769 specimens) formed by Edward Hawkins, formerly Keeper of the Department of Antiquities and author of *The Silver Coins of England*. The Bank of England donation (1877), which included the Cuff and Haggard medals, contributed also the completion of the series.

Of the extensive series of coins and medals of Medieval and Modern Europe, the Royal Collection presented by King George IV in 1823 forms a considerable part. The extensive collection of copper coins, tokens, and tickets of all countries formed by Dr. Freudenthal was acquired by purchase in 1870, and in 1906 Dr. F. Parkes Weber presented an important series of medieval and modern European coins and medals, numbering over 5,000 specimens. Acquisitions of less extent include the De Rin series of Venetian coins, purchased in 1861, and the collection of Swiss money presented by Count de Salis. The Townshend cabinet, another valuable collection of the coins of Switzerland, is also available for study at the British Museum.

Oriental Series

In 1834 William Marsden, the author of *Numismata Orientalia* and one of the first collectors of Eastern coins, presented his magnificent collection of Oriental money; but many extremely important additions, especially in the Indian section, have been made in recent years. In 1882 the collection of the India Office was transferred to the British Museum, and in 1888 the greater part of Sir Alexander Cunningham's celebrated collection of Bactrian and Indian coins was obtained by purchase. Sir Alexander's Hindu coins were subsequently presented to the Museum by his executors (1894). Sir Walter Elliot's cabinet of the coins of Southern India (presented in 1886), the Indian coins bequeathed by Pandit Bhagvanlal Indraji in 1889, and the selection from the Bleazby collection of Muhammadan coins, presented in 1911 by Mr. Henry Van den Bergh, are also acquisitions of importance, while the series of the coins of China, Japan, and the Far East, has grown rapidly since 1882, chiefly by the purchase of the Morse, Gardner, and Tamba collections.

General

The Department's Exhibition Room has not yet been restored after war damage. However it is now planned to have a comprehensive exhibition, including both coins and medals, in the vicinity of the departmental premises. In the meantime there is a select exhibit of Greek and Roman coins in the Greek and Roman Life Room; smaller temporary exhibits are made in the vestibule of the department. The Students' Room is intended primarily for serious study and research work, but it is also open for general enquiries and examination of coins from 10 a.m. to 12.30 p.m. and 2 p.m. to 4.30 p.m. each weekday (Saturday 10 a.m. to 12.30 p.m.) or by appointment. Advice may be supplied concerning coins and medals, but valuations cannot be given.

Department of Egyptian Antiquities

Office: Landing half-way up North-West Staircase

THE MUSEUM'S COLLECTION of Egyptian antiquities is one of the most representative in the world. Sculptures dating from almost every period in Egypt's history may be seen in two of the Department's galleries, one on the ground floor and one on the upper floor. Paintings of great interest both for the study of art and for the study of the incidents portrayed are shown in the Third Egyptian Room. A complete gallery (the Fourth Egyptian Room) is devoted to the display of objects illustrating various aspects of daily life, crafts of various kinds, furniture, toys, cosmetics, etc. The collection of mummies, human and animal, includes specimens dating from many different periods.

Apart from these objects the Department also houses the largest and finest library of documents written on papyrus which have survived from ancient Egypt. Among these papyri are several well-known literary works (e.g. the *Tale of the Two Brothers*, the *Eloquent Peasant*, the *Foredoomed Prince* and the *Blinding of Truth by Falsehood*), a number of collections of maxims (e.g. the so-called Wisdom of Ptahhotep, the Wisdom of Amenemope and the Wisdom of 'Onchsheshonqy), official documents (e.g. the tomb-robbery papyri, the accounts from the Pyramid temple of Neferirkare and the catalogue of temple-revenues in the Great Harris Papyrus), business documents (property agreements, etc.), scientific works (such as the London Medical Papyrus and the Rhind Mathematical Papyrus) and a very large collection of religious and magical works including the *Book of the Dead*, the *Book of What-is-in-the-Underworld*, oracles, interpretations of dreams, etc.

The objects exhibited in the galleries represent the finest pieces of the collection from the point of view of historical importance, artistic merit, state of preservation, and general interest. From the more common categories of objects a selection has been made of the more unusual examples as well as the more typical pieces illustrative of the range of such categories. Those which are not exhibited are held in the reserve collections. They are of importance mainly to the student. Much of the material is to be found in various excavation reports, specialised studies of particular classes of objects, in articles in learned periodicals, and in the official catalogues, handbooks and guides to individual rooms. Important new acquisitions are reported in the British Museum Quarterly.

Requests to see specified objects in the reserve collection should be made at the offices of the Department. Notice of the antiquities required by the student must be given at least one day before it is desired to study them.

Department of Western Asiatic Antiquities

*Office: Entrance in Coptic Gallery on Upper Floor
between King Edward VII Gallery and Egyptian Rooms*

Scope

THE DEPARTMENT OF Western Asiatic Antiquities was formed in 1955 to cover Mesopotamian and related material formerly included in the Department of Egyptian and Assyrian Antiquities. It contains antiquities from Sumer, Babylonia, Assyria (Iraq); Persia (Iran); Transcaucasia; Urartu, Hittite Asia Minor (Turkey); Palestine (Jordan and Israel); Syria, Lebanon, Arabia, and Phoenician colonies in the West Mediterranean.

The period it covers is from the Neolithic (or Late Stone) Age until the advent of Islam, during the 7th century A.D. Its most important possessions are its very large collection of cuneiform tablets and inscriptions, and the Assyrian palace reliefs which were discovered by the early excavators of Assyria, A. H. Layard and others, in the last century. During the period between the First and Second World Wars, the collections were greatly enlarged by participation in the excavations at Ur of the Chaldees, under the leadership of the late Sir C. L. Woolley.

Exhibitions

The Department contains the following exhibition galleries: *Ground Floor:* Assyrian Transept, Nimrud Gallery, Nimrud Central Saloon, Nineveh Gallery, Assyrian Entrance, Assyrian Saloon and Assyrian Basement, which are devoted to Assyrian sculpture and related antiquities. *Upper Floor:* Persian Landing, Hittite Room, Syrian Room, Room of Writing, Prehistoric Room and Babylonian Room.

In the Room of Writing there is an exhibition of inscriptions in various kinds of cuneiform and alphabetic script.

The Prehistoric Room contains material illustrating the cultures of Western Asia prior to 3000 B.C.

Students

A Students' Room, for the study of inscriptions and other antiquities in the Department's collections, is available on week-days from 10 a.m. to 4 p.m., and on Saturdays from 10 a.m. to 12 noon. Students wishing to study objects in it are desired to indicate their requirements in writing in advance.

Enquiries

Visitors with enquiries may submit them during the same hours. It is, however, regretted that the Staff of the Department cannot undertake for individuals or public bodies to:

1. Answer long and detailed questions, or carry out research.
2. Supply them with detailed advice on their studies or bibliographies.
3. Catalogue antiquities, or supply estimates of their financial value.

No responsibility is accepted for objects deposited in the Department for opinion, if they are unclaimed after six months.

Photography

Photographs of objects in the Department may be ordered. Black and white, and colour negatives exist for many, and prints of these may be seen during the above named hours in the Department Office.

Catalogues

Printed catalogues exist of the whole or parts of the Department's collections of cuneiform tablets, Assyrian reliefs, seals, carved ivories, and of the Treasure of the Oxus (Achaemenian gold work and jewellery). Many cuneiform texts have been published by the Trustees in the series *Cuneiform Texts . . . in the British Museum*.

The excavations of the British Museum at Carchemish and Ur, the latter jointly with The University Museum, Philadelphia, are published in official reports.

Popular booklets on the antiquities of the Department as well as albums of slides are available. A list may be obtained on request.

Department of Greek and Roman Antiquities

THE DEPARTMENT OF Greek and Roman Antiquities is concerned with the cultures of ancient Greece, Etruria and Rome. The collections comprise principally Minoan, Mycenaean, Greek, Cypriot, Etruscan and Roman antiquities, down to the edict of Milan in A.D. 313. Certain classes of Greek and Roman antiquities are, however, not found in this Department: coins are kept in the Department of Coins and Medals, papyri in the Department of Manuscripts, and the antiquities of Roman Britain in the Department of Prehistoric and Romano-British Antiquities.

The Ground Floor

The Department's ground-floor galleries re-opened in July 1969. They contain selected sculptures, vases, bronzes, terracottas and jewellery chronologically arranged to illustrate the development of art in classical lands from the Bronze Age to the Roman period. The exhibition includes sculptures from the Treasury of Atreus at Mycenae, the Temple of Apollo at Bassae, the Mausoleum and the Temple of Artemis at Ephesus. The sculptures of the Parthenon (the Elgin Marbles) are exhibited in the Duveen Gallery.

The Upper Floor

The Room of Greek and Roman Life contains select antiquities to illustrate the daily life of the Greeks and the Romans. In this gallery are also exhibitions of jewellery, silver plate and glass, wall-paintings and mosaics. Vases, bronzes, and terracottas are exhibited in other galleries on this floor.

Students

The Departmental Library, which is primarily a working library for the staff, is available to visitors who wish to study objects from the exhibited and reserve collections; it is open between 10 a.m. and 4.30 p.m. on week-days including Saturdays. Sculptures not on exhibition can normally be seen by special arrangement.

Enquiries

Visitors with enquiries may submit them between 10 a.m. and 4.30 p.m. The Department is, however, forbidden by regulation to give valuations; nor can they undertake research for members of the public, answer long and detailed questions, or catalogue collections of antiquities.

Photography

Photographs of objects in the Department may be ordered. In many cases negatives exist and prints will be made at small cost. In others, photographs will be taken specially by the Museum photographers. Those wishing to take their own photographs should consult the regulations on page 12.

Department of Medieval and Later Antiquities

Office: Entrance in Manuscript Saloon and the Indian Room (on first floor)

THE DEPARTMENT contains European antiquities dating from the Edict of Milan in A.D. 313 to the 19th century. The Department is responsible for the valuation of Treasure Trove (except for finds of coins) of this period, and in part for the administration of Treasure Trove legislation. A leaflet on Treasure Trove is published by the Director's Office.

Scope

The collections of the Department contains antiquities of the Early Christian, Byzantine, Migration, Carolingean, Medieval, Renaissance and later periods. The Renaissance collections include the Waddesdon Bequest (mainly silver-plate, jewellery, rock-crystals, and enamels). The collection of clocks and watches, which includes the Ilbert collection, now forms the most important historical collection in the world and illustrates the history of horology in all its aspects from the 15th to 20th century. The large collection of European glass and ceramics demonstrates the history of their development from the late Middle Ages to the 19th century. N.B. *The National collections of European sculpture, furniture, textiles, pewter, ironwork, and late 18th–19th century silver, are preserved at the Victoria and Albert Museum and not in this Department of the British Museum.*

Exhibitions

The European antiquities displayed in the King Edward VII Gallery will be removed from exhibition in phases during the period 1969–71 and will be re-exhibited in a sequence of galleries situated near the head of the main staircase.

THE STUDENTS' ROOM IN THE DEPARTMENT OF
GREEK AND ROMAN ANTIQUITIES

THE STUDENTS' ROOM IN THE DEPARTMENT OF
ORIENTAL ANTIQUITIES

STUDENTS' ROOM OF THE DEPARTMENT OF PREHISTORIC AND
ROMANO-BRITISH ANTIQUITIES

Facilities for Students

Bona Fide students are given every facility to study objects from collections, and they may use the Department's *Index Locorum* and Photographic Index. The National reference collection of Medieval pottery is now available for consultation. At least 48 hours notice in writing should be given by students wishing to study in the Department and, if not already known to the Keeper, they should submit a reference from a competent authority with their application. The Department is open to students between 10 a.m. and 4.30 p.m. on weekdays.

The Students' Room for Horology and Scientific Instruments is open on Tuesdays to Saturdays from 10 a.m. to 4.15 p.m.; a copy of the Regulations for its use and admission tickets may be obtained from the Keeper. The Students' Room, intended for use by students of the history of horology, by collectors and by practising members of the craft, including apprentices, offers facilities for between eight and twelve students in ideal conditions.

Enquiries

Specimens for identification and other enquiries will be received by post, or accepted from personal callers between 10 a.m. and 4.30 p.m. on weekdays. If it is not practicable for a qualified member of the staff to examine a specimen immediately, it may be left for subsequent collection or return with a report. Although every care will be taken of objects left in the custody of the Department, no liability is accepted in respect of them. Members of the staff are not permitted to give valuations and cannot answer questions which involve research.

Catalogues and handbooks produced by the Department are described in the official list *Books in Print*, published by the Trustees of the British Museum.

Department of Prehistoric and Romano-British Antiquities

Scope

In this Department are antiquities representing pre-farming communities from the whole of the Old World, European antiquities of the later Prehistoric periods, and a large Romano-British collection.

Exhibitions

Prehistoric and Romano-British antiquities are exhibited in the Central Saloon, the Roman Britain Room and the adjacent galleries in the area at the head of the main stairs.

Facilities for Students

The Department of Prehistoric and Romano-British Antiquities has two students' rooms. The Quaternary Room houses the Palaeolithic and Mesolithic collections, and there is accommodation there for students working on this material. Accommodation for students working on the Later Prehistoric and Romano-British collections is available in the new students' room near the Central Saloon. The Department's records and library are also housed in this room.

At least 48 hours' notice in writing should be given by students wishing to study in the Department, and, if not already known to the Keeper, they should submit a reference from a competent authority with their application.

The students' rooms are normally open between 10 a.m. and 4.45 p.m. except on Saturdays, Sundays and Public Holidays. Owing to the present shortage of staff, persons using the students' rooms are asked to accept occasional variations in the normal service.

Specimens for identification and other enquiries will be received by post, or accepted from personal callers between 10 a.m. and 4.30 p.m. on weekdays. If it is not practicable for a qualified member of the staff to examine a specimen immediately, it may be left for subsequent collection or return with a report. Although every care will be taken of objects left in the custody of the Department, no liability is accepted in respect of them. Members of the staff are not permitted to give valuations and cannot answer enquiries which involve research.

Catalogues and handbooks produced by the Department are described in the official list *Books in Print*, published by the Trustees of the British Museum.

Department of Oriental Antiquities

Office & Students' Room: Entrance on Upper Floor, King Edward VII Gallery

Scope

THE DEPARTMENT illustrates in its collections the civilisations of the Far East, South Asia and the Islamic lands. For the Far East and South Asia its responsibility begins with the Neolithic period, but in Western Asia and North Africa only from the Arab conquest in the 7th century A.D.

Exhibitions

Except for paintings and prints, first line material is always on exhibition in the King Edward VII Gallery, the Indian Room, and the Asiatic Saloon. Eastern paintings and drawings were not intended for permanent hanging like oil paintings, and are therefore shown in temporary exhibitions in the Gallery of Oriental Art, in which at least two complete changes are made each year. The collections of oriental paintings and prints are accessible to students and other interested visitors in the Departmental Students' Room, on the conditions summarised on page 16.

The reserve collections of antiquities are generally accessible either in the Students' Room or in the storage by appointment with the Department.

Oriental Paintings

The Department contains the National Collection of oriental paintings. Its foundation was laid by the purchase in 1881 of the large collection of Japanese and Chinese paintings formed in Japan by William Anderson, F.R.C.S. A catalogue was published in 1886. The most important accession ever made by the Department was the purchase in 1902 of the scroll painting on silk of the *Admonitions of the Preceptress,* attributed, at least since the 11th century, to the great Chinese master Ku K'ai-chih (*c.* 400 A.D.). This, the earliest surviving secular Chinese painting, is permanently exhibited. In 1913 the large collection of Japanese paintings formed by Arthur Morrison was presented by Sir Watkin Gwynne Evans, and this marked the establishment of a Sub-Department of Oriental Prints and Drawings, subsequently (1933) merged in the Department of Oriental Antiquities by union with the eastern ceramics and antiquities. Since 1913 the collections have been enlarged by the purchase of the Eumorfopoulos collection of Chinese paintings, bequests from O. C. Raphael and H. J. Oppenheim, and by numerous purchases, especially since 1950 by means of the fund established by P. T. Brooke Sewell. In 1919 the Department received a half share of the unique cache of Buddhist paintings and woodcuts recovered by Sir Aurel Stein from Ch'ien Fo Tung near Tun-huang in Kansu and dating from the 8th to the early 11th century. A catalogue by Mr. Arthur Waley was published in 1931.

Japanese and Chinese Woodcuts

The collection of Japanese woodcut prints is the most representative in Europe and includes an unrivalled series of actor prints by Sharaku, mainly the gift of Sir Ernest Satow, G.C.M.G.

The foundation of the Chinese woodcut collection was laid through the acquisition by Sir Hans Sloane of the collection of colour prints formed by Dr. Englebert Kaempfer (1692–93), historian of Japan. In both quality and quantity this collection is unmatched. A catalogue of the Japanese and Chinese woodcuts was published in 1916 and a further volume, retitled *Harunobu and his Age,* in 1964.

Indian and Persian Paintings

The basis of these collections consists of albums of miniatures and drawings acquired at different dates in the 19th century and transferred from the Oriental Printed Books and Manuscripts in 1920. The Indian collection has since been enriched by many acquisitions and especially from the bequest of part of the P. C. Manuk collection (1948) and by the purchase in 1955 of one half of the J. C. French collection. The importance of the Persian collection was much enhanced by the bequest of Sir Bernard Eckstein, Bt. (1948).

Students' Room

The Students' Room is open every day in the year, except Sundays, Good Friday, Christmas Day and Boxing Day. The hours are from 10 a.m. to 4 p.m., except on Saturdays, when they are from 10 a.m. to 1 p.m.

Department of Ethnography

Office: Entrance in Maudslay Room, leading off the Asiatic Saloon

THE COLLECTIONS of the Department of Ethnography include specimens from most tribal societies in Africa, America, Australia, Melanesia, Polynesia and much of Asia. There are important historical collections, among them the Cook Collection (Oceania and North America), Vancouver Collection (Oceania and North America), the Barrow Collection (Eskimo), Benin Collection (Nigeria), Torday Collection (Congo), Cooke-Daniels Collection (New Guinea).

In addition, the Department is responsible for the archaeology of the American continent, with representative collections from the Maya, Aztec, and other civilisations from Central America, the Mochica, Chimu and Inca civilisations from Peru and the Arawaks of the West Indies.

A small proportion (about 2 per cent) of the collections is exhibited in the public galleries, but visitors and students wishing to see specimens not on exhibition may apply to the Department for reasonable numbers of specimens from the reserve collections to be brought to the student for examination, subject to certain limitations imposed by fragility and inaccessibility. There are no restrictions on the photography or sketching of such specimens.

Certain selected groups of objects in constant demand, textiles, basketry, etc., are immediately available, and whenever possible, other specimens will be shown on application, but it is advisable to apply, if possible, a week in advance.

Specimens collected from store-rooms are available for study between 10 a.m. and 5 p.m. by visitors, and books in the Departmental Library are available for consultation in the studies by students.

The Departmental Staff will give all possible assistance and advice to students on the Museum's collections and on visitors' own specimens, but it is regretted that they cannot value specimens, undertake research for visitors or advise in detail on courses of study.

The Department holds a collection of some 10,000 photographic negatives and prints. These may be ordered from the Photographic Service in the Department, but visitors are referred to the Director's Office over matters of copyright, delivery dates and payment.

Note

The Department of Ethnography is preparing a temporary removal of its exhibited collections to specially converted premises at 6 Burlington Gardens, immediately behind the Royal Academy and close to Piccadilly Circus Underground Station. It hopes to open its first exhibitions in the autumn of 1970, and these will all be changing exhibitions, in order to make a much greater proportion of the collections accessible to the general public over a period; while only a selection of the cultures represented in the Department will be shown at any one time, these will be treated far more fully than is possible at present.

Department of Research Laboratory

THE RESEARCH LABORATORY is a Private Department of the Museum concerned with the scientific examination and conservation of antiquities and archaeological material.

The Departmental staff will give advice on matters of conservation.

Index